Encounters with God

The First, Second, and Third Epistles of JOHN and JUDE

Encounters with God Study Guide Series

The Gospel of Matthew

The Gospel of Mark

The Gospel of Luke

The Gospel of John

The Acts of the Apostles

The Book of Romans

The First Epistle of Paul the Apostle to the Corinthians

The Second Epistle of Paul the Apostle to the Corinthians

The Epistle of Paul the Apostle to the Galatians

The Epistle of Paul the Apostle to the Ephesians

The Epistle of Paul the Apostle to the Philippians

The Epistles of Paul the Apostle to the Colossians and Philemon

The First and Second Epistles of Paul the Apostle to the Thessalonians

The First and Second Epistles of Paul the Apostle to Timothy and Titus

The Epistle of Paul the Apostle to the Hebrews

The Epistle of James

The First and Second Epistles of Peter

The First, Second, and Third Epistles of John and Jude

The Revelation of Jesus Christ

Encounters with God

The First, Second, and Third Epistles of JOHN and JUDE

Contents

AN INTRODUCTION TO THE FIRST, SECOND, AND THIRD EPISTLES OF JOHN AND THE EPISTLE OF JUDE

This study guide covers four fairly short epistles: the first, second, and third epistles of John and the epistle of Jude. The letters have different authors, audiences, purposes, and styles, so we will deal with them individually.

The Epistles of John. First John and Hebrews are the only two New Testament letters that do not assign a proper name to the author and that do not begin with a greeting and introduction of author and recipients. Nevertheless, from the earliest decades, the church fathers—such as Clement of Alexandria, Origen, Tertullian, and Irenaeus—named the apostle John as the author of the books of John. First John does state that the author is among the eyewitness apostles to the life of Jesus and refers to "the Word of life" (1 John 1:1). This close alignment with the opening lines of the Gospel of John, as well as the letter's strong statements against the "antichrist" (1 John 2:18), "liars" (1 John 2:22), and "children of the devil" (1 John 3:10) all fit the gospel portrayal of the apostle John and reflect an intimate familiarity with the teachings of Jesus as they are presented in the gospels.

The style and content of 2 and 3 John are very similar to the first letter, suggesting the same author. The author refers to himself in these letters as "elder," a term of affection and church leadership, rather than apostle. By this time, few in the church would have doubted John's authority. Early church fathers claimed John the apostle as the author.

The three letters attributed to John likely were written from Ephesus, where John appears to have had a role similar to that of a modern-day bishop or district superintendent over seven major bodies of believers in Asia Minor. Church history states that John made his ministry headquarters in Ephesus after the ascension of Jesus and that he provided a home for Mary, the mother of Jesus, in that city. A major Christian church was established in

Ephesus as well as a discipleship school led by Tyrannus, where the apostle Paul taught for two years (Acts 19:9–10).

All of the letters were likely written between A.D. 85 and 95.

The first letter of John was written to help a church struggling under the influence of a heresy very similar to Gnosticism. This heresy had been taught throughout Asia Minor by a man named Cerinthus, and John's letter was likely intended for circulation throughout all of the churches in Asia Minor. The letter contends strongly that Jesus is both fully divine and fully human. It also proclaims that right belief goes hand-in-hand with right conduct and that true faith produces love, forgiveness, and effective prayer. The book reads more like a sermon than a letter and very likely was intended to be "preached" more than read. John presents three tests of authentic faith: obedience to God's law, love for God and His people, and a correct belief concerning Jesus Christ.

The second letter of John is addressed to the "elect lady and her children," which may have been the title given to a particular woman, or used as a figurative title for the church as a whole. The central message of this letter, which has only thirteen verses, is this: guard against inaccurate teaching and proclaim the truth. Again, as in 1 John, the issue being addressed has to do with the false teachings of traveling evangelists and teachers who were proclaiming that Christ was not God come in the flesh. John admonished the believers to use discernment and shun those who promoted heresy.

The third letter is addressed specifically to Gaius, apparently a trusted and influential leader in the church in Asia Minor. The main purpose of the letter, which has only fourteen verses, was to secure hospitality for legitimate traveling missionaries, especially Demetrius, and to promote enduring fellowship among genuine believers.

About the Author, John. The apostle John and his brother, James, were called "Sons of Thunder" by Jesus, apparently for their larger-than-life personalities as fishermen on the north shore of the Galilee. John was quick to leave his fishing nets and follow Jesus, and he and his brother—along with Peter—became something of an inner circle in which Jesus confided and revealed His identity as Messiah, through shared times of prayer, miracles, and revelation. John refers to himself in his writings as the "apostle whom Jesus loved," not that Jesus loved him in a peculiar or exalted way but rather that John's only claim before God the Father was this: Jesus loved me to the point of dying for me, and this I know without doubt. It is John who proclaims with a special emphasis in all of his writings the enormous privilege and responsibility Christians have when it comes to receiving God's love and extending the love of God to others.

The Epistle of Jude. The letter of Jude, only twenty-five verses in length, was written by Jude, "a bondservant of Jesus Christ, and brother of James" (Jude 1). The letter does not state the intended recipients, but from the content of the letter, we can conclude that the audience was well-versed in Old Testament Scripture. Jude commends the recipients for their knowledge of the Exodus (v. 5), angels (v. 6), and the destruction of Sodom and Gomorrah (v. 7). They also were acquainted with Jewish literature of the first century (vv. 9 and 14). There are no references to Gentiles. These factors have led church historians to believe the recipients were Jewish converts to Christianity who had been dispersed throughout Asia Minor.

Some scholars have speculated that the letter was written from Palestine or Egypt, but no setting has been identified with certainty.

The letter is very similar to 2 Peter and some believe Jude used Peter's letter as a reference or model. The letter was probably written sometime between A.D. 64 and 66, the same time frame for 2 Peter.

Jude's purpose was to warn the church against heretical teachers and divisive influences and to encourage believers to build themselves up in their "most holy faith." The book ends with one of the most beautiful statements of praise in the New Testament.

About the Author, Jude. From very early in the history of the church, Jude was recognized as not only the brother of James, the well-known leader of the church in Jerusalem, but, like James, as the half-brother of Jesus. He did not refer to himself as an apostle, but rested his authority first on his role as a servant to Jesus and then on his relationship to James.

Matthew 13:55 and Mark 6:3 refer to the brothers of Jesus and among the names given are James and Judas (or Jude). Why not state in his letter that he is the brother of Christ? Church fathers as far back as Clement of Alexandria (second century) have believed that the reason was Jude's humility. He saw himself as first and foremost a humble servant of Jesus. This humility may have been related to the fact that during their family life with Jesus they did not believe in Him (John 7:5). Their belief in Jesus as Savior and Lord came only after the Resurrection. Jude may not have regarded himself as a faithful brother, but he did desire to be a faithful follower.

AN OVERVIEW OF OUR STUDY OF THE FIRST, SECOND, AND THIRD EPISTLES OF JOHN AND THE EPISTLE OF JUDE

This study guide presents seven lessons drawn from the first, second, and third epistles of John and the epistle of Jude. The study guide elaborates upon the commentary included in the *Blackaby Study Bible*:

Lesson #1: Fellowship with the True Light

Lesson #2: The Love of the Father Bestowed on Us

Lesson #3: Dealing with Sin

Lesson #4: The Perfecting of Love

Lesson #5: Walking in the Truth of Christ

Lesson #6: Imitating and Doing Good

Lesson #7: Contending for the Faith

Personal or Group Use. These lessons are offered for personal study and reflection or for small-group Bible study. The study questions may be answered by an individual reader or used as a foundation for group discussion. A segment titled "Notes to Leaders of Small Groups" is included at the back of this book to help those leading a group study of this material.

Before you embark on this study, we encourage you to read in full the statement in the *Blackaby Study Bible* titled "How to Study the Bible." Our contention is that the Bible is unique among all literature. It is God's definitive word for humanity. The Bible is

- *inspired*—"God-breathed"

- *authoritative*—absolutely the final word on any spiritual matter

- *the plumb line of truth*—the standard against which all human activity and reasoning must be evaluated

The Bible is fascinating in that it has remarkable diversity but also remarkable unity. Its books were penned by a diverse assortment of authors representing a variety of languages and cultures, and it contains a number of literary forms. But the Bible's message, from cover to cover, is clear, consistent, and unified.

More than mere words on a page, the Bible is an encounter with God Himself. No book is more critical to your life. The very essence of the Bible is the Lord Himself.

The Holy Spirit speaks through the Bible. He also communicates during your time of prayer, in your life circumstances, and through the church. Read your Bible in an attitude of prayer, and allow the Holy Spirit to make you aware of God's activity in and through your personal life. Write down what you learn, meditate on it, and adjust your thoughts, attitudes, and behavior accordingly. Look for ways to apply the truth of God's Word to your circumstances and relationships every day. God is not random; He is orderly and intentional in the way He speaks to you.

Be encouraged—the Bible is *not* too difficult for the average person to understand if that person asks the Holy Spirit for help. (Furthermore, not even the most brilliant person can fully understand the Bible apart from the Holy Spirit's help!) God desires for you to know him and to know His Word. Every person who reads the Bible can learn from it. The person who will receive *maximum* benefit from reading and studying the Bible, however, is the person who:

- *is born again.* (John 3:3,5). Those who are born again and have received the gift of His Spirit have a distinct advantage in understanding the deeper truths of God's Word.

- *has a heart that desires to learn God's truth.* Your attitude greatly influences the outcome of Bible study. Resist the temptation to focus on what others have said about the Bible. Allow the Holy Spirit to guide you as you study God's Word for yourself.

- *has a heart that seeks to obey God.* The Holy Spirit teaches the most to those who have a desire to apply what they learn.

Begin your Bible study with prayer, asking the Holy Spirit to guide your thoughts and to impress upon you what is on God's heart. Then, make plans to adjust your life immediately to obey the Lord fully.

As you read and study the Bible, your purpose is not to *create* meaning, but to *discover* the meaning of the text with the Holy Spirit's guidance. Ask yourself, "What did the author have in mind? How was this applied by those who first heard these words?"

At times you may find it helpful to consult other passages of the Bible (made available in the center columns in the *Blackaby Study Bible*), or the commentary that is in the margins of the *Blackaby Study Bible*.

Keep in mind always that Bible study is not primarily an exercise for acquiring information but an opportunity for transformation. Bible study is your opportunity to encounter God and to be changed in His presence. When God speaks to your heart, nothing remains the same. Jesus said, "He who has ears to hear, let him hear" (Matt. 13:9). Choose to have ears that desire to hear!

The B-A-S-I-Cs of Each Study in This Guide. Each lesson in this study guide has five segments, using the word BASIC as an acronym. The word BASIC does not allude to elementary or simple but rather, to foundational. These studies extend the concepts that are part of the *Blackaby Study Bible* commentary and are focused on key aspects of what it means to be a Christ-follower in today's world. The BASIC acronym stands for:

B = *Bible Focus*. This segment presents the central passage for the lesson and a general explanation that covers the central theme or concern.

A = *Application for Today*. This segment has a story or illustration related to modern-day times, with questions that link the Bible text to today's issues, problems, and concerns.

S = *Supplementary Scriptures to Consider*. In this segment other Bible verses related to the general theme of the lesson are explored.

I = *Introspection and Implications*. In this segment, questions are asked that lead to deeper reflection about one's personal faith journey and life experiences.

C = *Communicating the Good News*. In this segment challenging questions point to ways the lesson's truth might be lived out and shared with others, whether to win the lost or build up the church.

LESSON #1

FELLOWSHIP
WITH THE TRUE LIGHT

Fellowship: companionship, including the sharing of common interests, goals, experiences, or views

B
Bible Focus

> *This is the message which we have heard from Him and declare to you, that God is light and in Him is no darkness at all. If we say that we have fellowship with Him, and walk in darkness, we lie and do not practice the truth. But if we walk in the light as He is in the light, we have fellowship with one another and the blood of Jesus Christ his Son cleanses us from all sin.*
>
> *If we say that we have no sin, we deceive ourselves, and the truth is not in us. If we confess our sins, He is faithful and just to forgive us our sins and to cleanse us from all unrighteousness. If we say that we have not sinned, we make Him a liar, and His word is not in us (1 John 1:5–10).*

John wasted little time in his message when it came to contradicting boldly three false claims of those who were spreading heresy in the early church:

- The false teachers claimed to have partnership with God, but they practiced and promoted beliefs God did not approve.

- The false teachers denied they had a sinful nature, but they did—everybody does!

- They denied that their conduct displeased God, but according to God's Word it did—thus, they accused God of lying.

These attributes of false teachers are evident throughout history. A false teacher nearly always claims to be doing God's work and to be a person of outstanding character who lives in accordance with God's Word. It takes careful discernment to see the lie in their message.

Taken as a whole, John's first letter gives thorough criteria for contrasting those who teach what is of God with those who do not:

THE MESSAGE THAT IS RIGHT BEFORE GOD IS:
1. Light—it guides people to truth, purity, and all that is right and holy (1 John 1:5,7; 2:9–10).

2. True (1 John 1:6; 2:4).

3. Life—both now and in eternity (1 John 1:2; 3:14).

4. Loving and compassionate (1 John 2:10; 3:11,18).

5. Enduring—forever (1 John 2:17).

6. Promotes faith (1 John 5:4,10).

7. An open acknowledgement of both the humanity of Christ and the divinity of Jesus (1 John 4:2; 1 John 4:15).

In sharp contrast, the message that is *not* right before God is:
1. Darkness—it contains or promotes things that are untrue, impure, and evil according to Scripture (1 John 1:5–6; 2:9,11).

2. A lie (1 John 1:6; 2:4).

3. Death-producing (1 John 3:14).

4. Hateful, fear-generating, and without compassion (1 John 2:11; 3:17; 4:18).

5. Temporal (1 John 2:17).

6. Something that promotes unbelief (1 John 5:10).

7. A denial of the divinity of Jesus and the humanity of Christ (1 John 2:22; 4:3).

Are you able to discern heresy from truth? Is your set of beliefs in full alignment with what is right before God?

One of the foremost heresies on the earth today is one that declares that no person is a sinner—people merely make mistakes that can be corrected and have flaws that should either be tolerated or improved. A person who justifies his behavior in such a way is a deluded embodiment of human pride, and sees no reason to believe in Jesus as Savior. Thus, such a person is very likely to die without any hope of salvation. To deny our sinful natures is to deceive ourselves about the full effects and consequences of sin.

The simple antidote for sin, John declared, was to confess it to God and be forgiven of it! The word confession in the Greek is a combination of two words, *homos* meaning "same" and *lego* meaning "to say." To confess is to say the same thing about sin that God says, and to see sin as deadly as God regards it. In today's language, we might say that confession is "owning up to" or "fully admitting" one's sinful nature, which separates a person from God. The good news, John wrote, is that when we do this and turn to God with faith in Christ Jesus, God *will* forgive sin and cleanse all things that are standing in the way of our full reconciliation with Him.

Confession is not limited to admitting our sins to God. It is also something we must do in our relationships. We must own up to our trespasses against others and, acting on the faith we have in Christ Jesus, seek full reconciliation with those we have hurt.

To do this—to confess our sins against God and man, to express our faith in Christ Jesus, and to be forgiven and restored—is what it means to have genuine *fellowship* with both God and man.

Are you in full fellowship with God? With other people?

A
Application for Today

"But I'm not dirty!" the little boy argued with his mother. "Normally you just tell me to wash my hands before dinner, not take a bath."

"But today you need a bath before dinner," Mom noted matter-of-factly.

"No, I don't!" the boy continued to protest as he pointed down to the nearly clean front of his t-shirt. "Just look, my shirt hardly has anything on it at all."

"You've been playing baseball, right?" Mom asked.

"Yes," the boy said.

"And sliding into second base, right?" Mom asked again.

"Yes," the boy said, "and I was safe both times!"

Mom led her son to a full-length mirror, turned him around, and handed him a hand mirror so he could see the backside of his clothes. They were mud-caked from the neckline of his t-shirt to the hem of his jeans.

"And what do we call this that we see in the mirror?" Mom asked.

The boy paused for a moment and then replied with enthusiasm, thinking perhaps he had found a solution, "Those are *clothes* that need a bath. But I don't!"

Do you really believe that you are 100 percent clean before God? On what basis?

What does it mean to you to be cleansed from all unrighteousness?

Is it time for a spiritual bath?

S
Supplementary Scriptures to Consider

John opened his gospel with words about light and darkness:

> In the beginning was the Word, and the Word was with God,
> and the Word was God. He was in the beginning with God. All

things were made through Him, and without Him nothing was made that was made. In Him was life, and the life was the light of men. And the light shines in the darkness, and the darkness did not comprehend it (John 1:1–5).

• What does the truth of God's Word reveal about sin (darkness)? In other words, what is the truth about sin?

• How did the life and death of Jesus confront sin?

• Why don't people recognize their sinfulness and their need to confront their sin and be cleansed of it?

Jesus said this about Himself:

Then Jesus spoke to them again, saying, "I am the light of the world. He who follows Me shall not walk in darkness, but have the light of life" (John 8:12).

• When we follow Jesus, we know which way to go so we might have abundant and eternal life. In what ways has Jesus revealed to you the right way to live? How do you rely upon God to show you what is right and wrong?

• What is the end result of making right decisions and choices according to God's Word?

John wrote in his first letter that those who live in the light will love other people:

> The darkness is passing away, and the true light is already shining. He who says he is in the light, and hates his brother, is in darkness until now. He who loves his brother abides in the light, and there is no cause for stumbling in him. But he who hates his brother is in darkness and walks in darkness, and does not know where he is going, because the darkness has blinded his eyes (1 John 2:8–11).

- What does it really mean to *love* a brother in Christ Jesus? Is this the same love we are to have for those who are unsaved?

- How is loving a brother in Christ different than loving God, or is it different?

- John contended that a person cannot love God and hate his brothers simultaneously. Have you ever encountered someone who claimed to love God and be a Christian, yet was filled with hatred toward a specific person or group of people? How did you deal with that person? What was the outcome?

- In what ways is it difficult for a person to recognize his own level of hatred? What about hatred that comes in the guise of racial prejudice or socioeconomic bias?

- A person once said, "I only hate people who are hateful." Would that line of argument be acceptable to John? Why?

James wrote about light from a slightly different perspective, claiming that there is no wavering or confusion in those things that God imparts to us:

> Every good gift and every perfect gift is from above, and comes down from the Father of lights, with whom there is no variation or shadow of turning (James 1:17).

- In what ways is loving one's brothers a part of God's good and perfect gift to us? (Note: a good gift is a gift that produces good in us and enables us to show good to others; a perfect gift is a gift that makes us whole, individually and as the body of Christ.)

I
Introspection and Implications

1. Do you ever wish you could just walk away and forget some people who say they are your Christian brothers or sisters? Is walking away from some people who claim to be in the church an act of hating them? Is rejection of a Christian brother or sister an expression of hatred?

2. In what ways do you struggle to own up to your own sin and confess it to God? In what ways is it difficult for a person to recognize his or her own errors?

3. Is it easier in some ways to love your Christian brothers and sisters if you see this as a way of expressing your love for God?

4. In what ways is it difficult to remain in the light and not wander into the darkness of error and sin?

C
Communicating the Good News

Summarize the gospel message in twenty-five words or less:

Is the message you have written above fully in alignment with John's criteria for what is a right message before God?

Does it matter whether this message is delivered with an attitude of love?

LESSON #2

THE LOVE OF THE FATHER BESTOWED ON US

*Bestowed: presented or poured out
in lavish abundance, without recall*

B
Bible Focus

> *Behold what manner of love the Father has bestowed on us,*
> *that we should be called children of God! Therefore the world*
> *does not know us, because it did not know Him. Beloved, now*
> *we are children of God; and it has not yet been revealed what*
> *we shall be, but we know that when He is revealed, we shall*
> *be like Him, for we shall see Him as He is. And everyone who*
> *has this hope in Him purifies himself, just as He is pure. . . .*
>
> *Beloved, let us love one another, for love is of God; and*
> *everyone who loves is born of God and knows God. He who*
> *does not love does not know God, for God is love. In this the*
> *love of God was manifested toward us, that God has sent his*
> *only begotten Son into the world, that we might live through*
> *Him. In this is love, not that we loved God, but that He loved*
> *us and sent his Son to be the propitiation for our sins. Be-*
> *loved, if God so loved us, we also ought to love one another*
> *(1 John 3:1–3, 4:7–11).*

What an awesome thing it is to believe that the God who created the universe in all of its vastness and diversity, the God who holds all truth, wisdom, and power in His hands, the God who is infinite and eternal might love *one human being*—you! The concept was nearly overwhelming to John. It should be equally overwhelming to us.

We can never fully comprehend why God would love us even a little, much less comprehend the fullness of God's love for us. Nor can we fully fathom what it means to be a beloved child of God—not a mere creation of God, but a beloved *child*. Nevertheless, our ability to love other people, purify ourselves, and become more like Jesus, are dependent upon our ability to grasp what it means to be a beloved child.

When John wrote, "God is love," he was describing God's character and the motivation for all God's actions. He was not equating God *with* love—in other words, God is love, but love is not God. Rather, John was declaring that God cannot act in any way other than a loving way—love is the fore-most description of His nature. The supreme manifestation of God's love was the coming of Himself in the form of Jesus to be the sacrifice required for forgiveness of sins. God Himself invaded time and space to die for us, so that one day we might transcend time and space and live forever in a fully reconciled relationship with Him.

One of the amazing truths John declared was this: we will be like Him. We are not like Christ Jesus at present. We can't even begin to imagine fully what it will be like to be like Jesus. Nevertheless, once we see Him, we shall become like Him. God's love will perfect us fully the moment we are before His throne.

What is it that love does for us in the here and now?

Love is at the root of our *wanting* to be like Jesus. It is at the root of what enables us to become like Him. As Jesus lives in us and His love permeates our lives, He empowers us to love others. We have a growing desire to be like Jesus in all ways, including the way Jesus loved. The person who truly knows that He is a beloved child of Almighty God wants to live in a way that is pleasing to God, and part of what pleases God is the way we love our fellow brothers and sisters in Christ. There is to be no sibling rivalry in the family of God!

John went so far as to say that if we do not love others, we don't really love God. To love God is to love as He loved—fully, openly, and without measure. The only way we can begin to love as God loved is to allow God's love to flow into us and *through* us. We must never think we have a corner on God's love. His love is meant to be poured out on all mankind.

In what ways is this passage from 1 John challenging to you?

What does it mean to *you* to know that you are a beloved child of the Creator of all things?

A
Application for Today

"Oh, no!" the little girl said when she heard that Aunt Lou was coming for a visit and was just minutes away from her arrival at their house.

"What do you mean?" her mother asked. "You love Aunt Lou."

"I *do* love Aunt Lou," the little girl replied, heading for her bedroom.

"Then why did you say, 'oh, no?'"

"I'm not ready for her to come. I need to put on lots more clothes."

"Why?" her mother asked, with no clue as to what her daughter meant. She followed her daughter to her bedroom and watched as she began to put on two sweaters and then a coat. "Why *are* you doing this? Mom asked again.

"Aunt Lou hugs me so tight and for so long I almost break in two!"

Mom laughed. "Well, she loves you!"

"I know," the little girl said, "but I think maybe she loves me a little too much!"

Do you ever feel as if someone is loving you too much?

Is it possible to be loved by God too much?

What is it we feel obligated to do in the face of great love? Why is that a challenge to us?

S
Supplementary Scriptures to Consider

In his second letter John underscored his admonition that our response to God's outpouring of love and His adoption of us as His beloved children is that we walk in obedience to God's commandments, just as a child obeys his parents.

> This is love, that we walk according to His commandments.
> This is the commandment, that as you have heard from the
> beginning, you should walk in it (2 John 6).

• Do you obey those who are in authority over you whether they love you or not? Is there a greater imperative to obey when you know someone in authority loves you deeply?

• Are a rebellious heart and a failure to *feel loved* connected? How so?

• Does love give a person a "want to" when it comes to obeying God's commandments? How so?

• Do we obey God because He loves us or because we love Him—or both?

John admonished the church to respond to God's bestowal of love and choose both to love God in return and pursue the things of God, rather than love the world and pursue the things of the world:

> Do not love the world or the things in the world. If anyone loves the world, the love of the Father is not in him. For all that is in the world—the lust of the flesh, the lust of the eyes, and the pride of life—is not of the Father but is of the world. And the world is passing away, and the lust of it, but he who does the will of God abides forever (1 John 2:15–17).

• John identified three characteristics of wordly (or "fleshly") living that are in sharp contrast to a display of God's love:

  1. *Lust of the flesh* (insatiable pursuit of things thought to meet basic human needs and drives)—the love of pleasure

  2. *Lust of the eyes* (insatiable greed)—the love of possessions

  3. *The pride of life* (a desire for fame and power)—the love of importance

What or who is the focus in each of these three areas of desire? What or who is the focus of love? Why can't a love for the things of this world and a love for God coexist?

- Does knowing that the lusts of this world are temporary make it easier to deal with them and deny them? Why?

- What is the challenge of loving a person and not lusting?

- What is the challenge in admiring something greatly but not insisting on ownership of it?

- How might a person value himself without demanding that others value him?

John sharply contrasted the natures of the beloved children of God and of those who have not yet received God's outpouring of love and forgiveness:

> In this the children of God and the children of the devil are manifest: Whoever does not practice righteousness is not of God, nor is he who does not love his brother. For this is the message that you heard from the beginning, that we should love one another, not as Cain who was of the wicked one and murdered his brother. And why did he murder him? Because his works were evil and his brother's righteous. Do not marvel, my brethren, if the world hates you. We know that we have passed from death to life, because we love the brethren. He who does not love his brother abides in death. Whoever hates his brother is a murderer, and you know that no murderer has eternal life abiding in him (1 John 3:10–15).

• John equated hatred with murder. What is it that we "kill" when we hate another person?

• How does one person's goodness create hatred in another person? Why is it the fleshly human tendency to hate others who appear to have greater favor from God?

• Reread Genesis 4:1–15. Note that Cain was upset that God respected Abel and his offering. Note also that God said to Cain, "If you do well, will you not be accepted? And if you do not do well, sin lies at the door. And its desire is for you, but you should rule over it" (v. 6). Cain could have chosen to change his offering, but instead he killed his brother. What keeps a person from refusing to do what is right? Can you cite an example of a person who refused to do what he knew was the right thing to do, and instead persecuted or spoke out against the godly person who was doing the right thing? Does denunciation of what is right and loving inevitably lead to open hatred against those who are doing what is right and loving?

I
Introspection and Implications

1. Do you fully believe you are loved by God? Why or why not? If you do not feel fully loved by God, what would it take for you to grow in these feelings? Is it enough just to know you are loved by God, or do you need to *experience* God's love *emotionally*?

2. Are you a loving person? If so, what evidence do you cite? If not, what stands in the way of your becoming a loving person?

3. Do you love all people equally? What are the challenges you face in loving others as God loves?

4. Is it possible for a person to fully love others if he or she hasn't first received God's love?

C
Communicating the Good News

In what ways is experiencing God's love a prerequisite for being an effective witness of God's love to other people?

In what ways might a Christian communicate God's love without using words?

LESSON #3

DEALING WITH SIN

*Sin: anything that separates us from
full reconciliation and the blessings of God*

B
Bible Focus

> *My little children, these things I write to you, so that you may not sin. And if anyone sins, we have an Advocate with the Father, Jesus Christ the righteous. And He Himself is the propitiation for our sins, and not for ours only but also for the whole world. . . .*
>
> *Whoever commits sin also commits lawlessness, and sin is lawlessness. And you know that He was manifested to take away our sins, and in Him there is no sin. Whoever abides in Him does not sin. Whoever sins has neither seen Him nor known Him.*
>
> *Little children, let no one deceive you. He who practices righteousness is righteous, just as He is righteous. He who sins is of the devil, for the devil has sinned from the beginning. For this purpose the son of God was manifested, that He might destroy the works of the devil. Whoever has been born of God does not sin, for his seed remains in him; and he cannot sin, because he has been born of God (1 John 2:1–2; 3:4–9).*

At first reading this passage may give a person great concern. Most people immediately respond, "I still sin from time to time! How can I possibly live a sin-free life?" A closer examination gives cause for hope.

Note that John wrote that he is writing that the believers "may not sin." He immediately followed this by writing, "And if anyone sins." There were false teachers proclaiming that knowledge had made them perfect and sinless. John refuted the possibility of this (1 John 1:8,10). Other false teachers contended that sin didn't really matter because sin did not affect a person's spiritual soul; it only marred a person's body, mind, or emotions, all of which were temporal. John saw no separation between the effects of sin on the outer body and the inner spirit; sin infected the whole of a person. Further, John argued that everyone sins, including the Christian, and that God graciously extends forgiveness to all who will confess their sins and declare their faith in Christ Jesus (1 John 1:9).

John did not deny the possibility of sin in the Christian. Rather, he argued that the Christian does not engage in a habitual lifestyle of sin. Just as righteousness is subject to practice, so the sin to which John refers is one that is repetitive. His statements about sin and righteousness refer to a settled character, an engrained propensity, and habitual practice.

John called the attention of the church to the *incongruity* of sin in the Christian, not the *impossibility* of sin. The Christian who abides in Christ Jesus will not *want* to sin, will do his utmost to avoid sin and to obey God's commandments, will intentionally seek God's help in avoiding temptations and withstanding impulses to sin, and will desire to reflect the nature of Jesus at all times and in all situations.

John stated that the Christian who has been born of God has been imparted the "seed" of God—he or she has become God's own child. Those who are of God's seed will act as children of God, not as children of the devil. One cannot abide in Christ and seek to become more and more like Jesus and, at the same time, act in ways that are more and more like the devil.

The good news is that when a Christian does sin, he has an advocate with the Father. The word advocate comes from the Greek *parakletos*, which literally means "one called alongside." This was a courtroom term in Greece for a person who defended and pleaded the cause of a person on trial. Jesus is the one who intercedes before God the Father on behalf of the sinner. The word is also used to describe the work of the Holy Spirit, who speaks to the Christian continually in the inner recesses of the believer's heart, convicting and pleading with the Christian to turn from sin, seek God's forgiveness, and to establish new patterns of behavior. When we sin, we can trust Jesus to be our mediator with God and to declare that, on the basis of our relationship with Him, we are to be forgiven.

John also said that Jesus is the propitiation for our sin. This word refers to full appeasement or satisfaction. Jesus has already paid the price for *all* of our sin—past, as well as present. Jesus does not ask God to declare us innocent but rather, on the basis of His sacrifice, to declare that we are pardoned.

Is there any license for a Christian to choose to sin? No.

Is there automatic forgiveness for the Christian, with no need for confession of sin and repentance? No.

Is there ongoing forgiveness for Christians who own up to their sins and seek God's mercy? Absolutely.

What is at stake are the *behavioral habits* a Christian chooses and continues to pursue. We each must ask ourselves about each of the habits of our life, "Does this draw me closer to God and help me become more like Jesus?" If the answer is no, we must change that habit!

Are there patterns of behavior in your life that you believe you must change? How will you pursue making those changes?

A
Application for Today

In a discussion of this passage, a man once admitted in a small-group setting, "This idea of living a sinless life is what kept me away from the church for twenty years." The leader of the group asked him to expand on his statement. The man said:

"I grew up in a church that believed once you were saved, you had to live a sinless life. If you committed even one sin, you were back to square one and needed to be saved again. I saw people getting 'resaved' again and again, year after year. Those who got tired of going to the altar to get 'resaved,' eventually took a stance that they had not sinned—at least not to a degree that they needed resaving. They lived with a certain amount of guilt, nevertheless, because they knew deep within that they *had* sinned. They were miserable people who tended to judge others harshly in order to elevate their own goodness—in their own eyes, at least. Others, like me, got tired of the whole idea that we had to *try* to do the impossible.

"In the end, the people in the church where I grew up had very little joy. There was very little emphasis on growing spiritually. All of the focus seemed to be on sin, and very little of it on what it meant to be a vibrant, loving, faithful servant of Christ.

"When I did come back to the church, I purposefully chose a church that placed greater emphasis on what it meant to be a saint, rather than emphasis on the inevitability that I would always be a sinner."

Respond to this man's statement. Have you had a similar experience?

Have you ever felt that you were a hopeless case when it came to committing sin?

How might a preoccupation with sin issues keep a person from growing spiritually?

S
Supplementary Scriptures to Consider

Jesus said:

> "Beware of false prophets, who come to you in sheep's
> clothing, but inwardly they are ravenous wolves. You will
> know them by their fruits. Do men gather grapes from thorn-
> bushes or figs from thistles? Even so, every good tree bears
> good fruit, but a bad tree bears bad fruit. A good tree cannot

bear bad fruit, nor can a bad tree bear good fruit. Every tree
that does not bear good fruit is cut down and thrown into the
fire. Therefore by their fruits you will know them"
(Matt. 7:15–20).

• How does this passage from the gospels relate to what John wrote to the
church about the practice of righteousness or lawlessness?

• In what ways do you *not* want others to judge you according to your
behavior?

• What makes a person good? What makes the works of that person's life
good?

John regarded full obedience to God's commands as a sign that God's love had been perfected in a believer:

> Now by this we know that we know Him, if we keep His commandments. He who says, "I know Him," and does not keep His commandments, is a liar, and the truth is not in him. But whoever keeps His word, truly the love of God is perfected in him. By this we know that we are in Him. He who says he abides in Him ought himself also to walk just as He walked (1 John 2:3–6).

• John was not referring to a head knowledge of God or His commandments. He was referring to knowing Jesus, and because the same Spirit indwells us that indwelt Christ Jesus, our knowing of Jesus causes us to live as Jesus lived: in full agreement with all God's commandments. What is the difference between knowing a commandment is the right thing to do and desiring to keep a commandment because Christ's Spirit is within us?

• The word *perfected* means *brought to fullness or completion*. For love to be perfected in us, we must *live out* the love in our hearts; we must behave in a loving way. How does keeping God's commandments complete our beliefs about God's love? Is this a matter of aligning belief with behavior?

- The popular phrase, "What would Jesus do?" is one John might have stated this way: "How would Jesus love?" A second related question is this: "How did love compel Jesus to act?" Is this the way we are to act?

I
Introspection and Implications

1. John wrote that sin is lawlessness and that those who commit sin commit lawlessness. The law refers to the law of God. Law-obeying—doing what is righteous—means routinely, regularly, and faithfully living in accordance with the commands of God. The result is the establishment of a pattern of godly behavior. Lawlessness is the flip side: routinely, regularly, and consistently doing what is rebellious and ungodly. It is the establishment of a pattern of behavior that is contrary to God's commandments. Think back to your life before you accepted Jesus as your Savior. In what ways did you commit lawlessness?

2. Do you believe it is ever possible for a person to become so spiritually mature that he or she *cannot* sin? Is it possible to become so spiritually mature that a person *will not* sin? Is it possible to become so spiritually mature that a person will have no *desire* to sin?

3. A young man once said, "I was in the principal's office about fifty times when I was in third grade, and then one day I decided I was tired of sitting in the principal's office. I stopped doing the things that resulted in my being sent to the principal's office. It wasn't anything my teacher said or the principal said. It was something I decided." To what extent does a person need to *decide* to change patterns of behavior that are not in keeping with God's commandments? How does our Advocate, the Holy Spirit, help us follow through on that decision? To what degree is the establishment of a new pattern of godly behavior our responsibility? God's responsibility?

4. To what degree does a person need ongoing "cleansing" of unrighteousness? How do you go about gaining that cleansing?

C
Communicating the Good News

Is it possible to address the good news of salvation in Christ Jesus without mentioning sin?

Once a person has been saved from the consequences related to their sinful nature, does that person ever need to be resaved?

LESSON #4

THE PERFECTING OF LOVE

*Love: to give to another what is for the
eternal benefit of that person*

B
Bible Focus

> *By this we know love, because He laid down His life for us. And we also ought to lay down our lives for the brethren. But whoever has this world's goods, and sees his brother in need, and shuts up his heart from him, how does the love of God abide in him?*
>
> *My little children, let us not love in word or in tongue, but in deed and in truth. And by this we know that we are of the truth, and shall assure our hearts before Him. For if our heart condemns us, God is greater than our heart, and knows all things. Beloved, if our heart does not condemn us, we have confidence toward God. And whatever we ask we receive from Him, because we keep His commandments and do those things that are pleasing in His sight. And this is His commandment: that we should believe on the name of His Son Jesus Christ and love one another, as He gave us commandment. . . .*
>
> *Love has been perfected among us in this: that we may have boldness in the day of judgment; because as He is, so are we in this world. There is no fear in love; but perfect love casts out fear, because fear involves torment. But he who fears has not been made perfect in love. We love Him because He first loved us (1 John 3:16–23; 4:17–19).*

John did not only call the church to love but to the *perfection* of love! This perfection comes not by merely saying "I love you"—although that certainly should not be neglected—but by *showing* "I love you" in acts of sacrificial giving.

To show love is not to show mere kindness, though that is certainly beneficial.

To show love is not limited to expressions of mercy and forgiveness, although these are great acts of love.

To show love in its perfected form is to give something to someone else that is for his or her *eternal* benefit. Giving that has eternity attached to it is always sacrificial because it requires yielding ourselves fully to God's eternal plan and inviting God to use us to show His love to others. In this sense, it truly means laying down one's own life—one's personal desires, limitations, inhibitions, hesitancies, feelings, fears, and motives—and allowing God to provide all guidance in what to say, when to say it, how to say it, as well as what to do, when to act, and how to act. Sacrificial giving for eternal benefit is made possible only when we yield ourselves fully to God and allow Him to use us as a vessel through which He pours His love.

Sacrificial giving *always* points toward God's love and to the mercy, forgiveness, wholeness, and grace born of His love.

John assured the church that anytime a person asked God to use him or her to show love to another person, God would quickly answer that prayer!

To show sacrificial love is to invite the Holy Spirit to give us boldness to:

- give the gospel message to a person who has never heard it or has not yet received it.

- admonish a Christian to trust God fully and resist all temptations.

- pray with confidence for a person to be healed and made whole.

- encourage a person to grow in his or her relationship with the Lord.

- and many other acts that go beyond what we feel comfortable in saying or doing but know that God still desires for us to do or say in His name.

When our love becomes a reflection of God's own perfect love, love is made whole or complete in us.

Are you willing to give yourself completely to God so that He might pour His love to others through you?

A
Application for Today

"I love Jennie," a young man told his spiritual mentor, "but I can't seem to get that message through to her. She just doesn't seem to believe me."

"What have you tried?" the mentor asked.

"I sent a card and signed it 'love.' I told her one night that I loved her, but it was right after she had just cooked a big bowl of spaghetti and meatballs for me, and I'm not sure she knew that I meant what I said. I've tried using some of the other love languages I've read about. I spent an hour with her last week just conversing with her about what she wanted to talk about. I gave her a little heart necklace. But I still don't think she understands that I really, really really love her."

"Why don't you pray about this?" the mentor suggested. But then he quickly added, "Ask God to show you whether you really do love her."

"But I do love her," the young man protested.

"Talk to God about what you are willing to give up completely for her sake, or what you are willing to give sacrificially to Jennie. Do you love her for what her love might mean to you and what she might give to you, or do you deeply desire to give to her?"

"Alright," the young man said. He went home and that evening, got down on his knees and prayed as his mentor had suggested. The next day he returned to report, "I prayed as you suggested."

"And?" the mentor asked.

"I guess I don't really love Jennie as much as I thought I did," he said. "I started to tell God what I was willing to give up for Jennie's sake, and I came up with very little. The truth hurts, but I really don't want to give up very much of my time for her. I don't want to give up going out with my guy friends. If she wanted me to go with her to her Thursday night Bible study, or if she asked me to give up some of my favorite habits, I don't think I'd agree. The more I prayed, the more I realized that I wanted Jennie to love me so *she* could give to *me*. In truth, there is very little I am willing to *sacrifice* for her."

"You're a brave man to admit that to yourself," his mentor responded. "When you really love another person, you *want* to give everything you have so that person can become all they were designed to be by God their Creator."

Are you willing to be a *sacrificial* giver?

S
Supplementary Scriptures to Consider

John regarded expressions of love as being very practical and observable:

> If someone says, "I love God," and hates his brother, he is a liar; for he who does not love his brother whom he has seen, how can he love God whom he has not seen? And this commandment we have from Him: that he who loves God must love his brother also (1 John 4:20–21).

• Who is your brother? In what ways must we see a person as God sees that person?

• How do we love our brothers and sisters in Christ as God loves them?

John's letter repeats a message found in John's gospel. A message Jesus gave to John and the other apostles at the time of the Last Supper became the message John passed on to the church:

> These things I have spoken to you, that My joy may remain in you, and that your joy may be full. This is My commandment, that you love one another as I have loved you. Greater love has no one than this, than to lay down one's life for his friends. You are My friends if you do whatever I command you. No longer do I call you servants, for a servant does not know what his master is doing; but I have called you friends, for all things that I heard from My Father I have made known to you. You did not choose Me, but I chose you and appointed you that you should go and bear fruit, and that your fruit should remain, that whatever you ask the Father in My name He may give you. These things I command you, that you love one another (John 15:11–17).

• Give several examples of what it means to "lay down your life" for another person, apart from physical death.

- What does it mean to be called a friend by God? By other people? What do friends do for each other?

- Do you have a sense that you have been chosen by God? Appointed by God? How so? For what purpose?

- What does it mean to you to bear fruit that remains?

- How is fulfilling God's commands essential to having our prayers answered?

John called upon the church to be bold both in declaring *how* a person is born of God, and in manifesting love through obedience and faith:

> Whoever believes that Jesus is the Christ is born of God, and everyone who loves Him who begot also loves him who is begotten of Him. By this we know that we love the children of God, when we love God and keep His commandments. For this is the love of God that we keep His commandments. And His commandments are not burdensome. For whatever is born of God overcomes the world. And this is the victory that has overcome the world—our faith. Who is he who overcomes the world, but he who believes that Jesus is the Son of God (1 John 5:1–5).

• To be begotten means to be a child who is completely like its Father in all ways. John said we are fully like our heavenly Father when we love *as* He loves, love *what* He loves, and keep His commandments that were given to us because He loves us.

Describe the way God loves:

Identify several things God loves:

- Do you ever find the commandments of God burdensome? How so? What can be done to keep them from being burdensome? Does an attitude of godly love turn an act of obedience from chore to privilege?

John admonished the church to base its boldness in loving others upon the certainty of having received the gift of eternal life:

> This is He who came by water and blood—Jesus Christ; not only by water, but by water and blood. And it is the Spirit who bears witness, because the Spirit is truth. For there are three that bear witness in heaven: the Father, the Word, and the Holy Spirit; and these three are one. And there are three that bear witness on earth: the Spirit, the water, and the blood; and these three agree as one. If we receive the witness of men, the witness of God is greater; for this is the witness of God which He has testified of His Son. He who believes in the Son of God has the witness in himself; he who does not believe God has made Him a liar, because he has not believed the testimony that God has given of His Son. And this is the testimony: that God has given us eternal life, and this life is in His Son. He who has the Son has life; he who does not have the Son of God does not have life. These things I have written to you who believe in the name of the Son of God, that you may know that you have eternal life, and that you may continue to believe in the name of the Son of God (1 John 5:6–13).

- John declared that Father, Son, and Holy Spirit all bear witness to the truth of God's commandments and the mercy of God's love. On earth,

John said, we also have three witnesses. We receive this witness by the Holy Spirit speaking to our spirit, by the newness we experience at baptism, and by an assurance that the shed blood of Christ was on our behalf. How have each of these witnesses impacted your walk with the Lord?

The Spirit speaking to your heart about Jesus—

Your willful act of being baptized as an outward sign that inwardly you were dying to old self and rising as a new creation—

Believing that the blood of Jesus was shed on your behalf—

• Do you feel fully confident that your sins have been forgiven? Do you have full confidence that an eternal home awaits you in heaven?

• How does your belief in what God has done for you translate into active love for other people?

I
Introspection and Implications

1. Have you ever seen a fellow Christian in need and shut your heart to him or her? How did you feel? What was the outcome?

2. John wrote, "There is no fear in love; but perfect love casts out fear, because fear involves torment. But he who fears has not been made perfect in love." Have you ever been afraid to show God's love to another person? How does fear keep a person from reaching the perfection of love that God desires for His children to experience?

3. John wrote, "We love Him because He first loved us." How was this truth manifested in your life? How might your sharing Christ with another person be God's way of *showing* His love for that person *through you?*

C
Communicating the Good News

In what ways is an expression of God's love the greatest evangelistic tool of all?

How can we infuse love into all of our evangelistic outreaches and messages? Why is it important that we do so?

Do you have a strong sense that Jesus already loves the unsaved person to whom you feel compelled to share the gospel? Does this add boldness to your presentation of the gospel? How so?

LESSON #5

WALKING IN THE TRUTH OF CHRIST

Antichrist: against Christ—when lower case, "antichrist" refers to a doctrine, belief, behavior, or message that is against Christ; when upper-case, "Antichrist" refers to the personification of one who, in the last days, opposes Christ and claims to be greater than Christ

B
Bible Focus

> *To the elect lady and her children, whom I love in truth,*
> *and not only I, but also all those who have known the truth,*
> *because of the truth which abides in us and will be with us*
> *forever. . . .*
>
> *I rejoiced greatly that I have found some of your children*
> *walking in truth, as we received commandment from the*
> *Father. . . .*
>
> *For many deceivers have gone out into the world who do*
> *not confess Jesus Christ as coming in the flesh. This is a*
> *deceiver and an antichrist. Look to yourselves, that we do not*
> *lose those things we worked for, but that we may receive a full*
> *reward.*
>
> *Whoever transgresses and does not abide in the doctrine of*
> *Christ does not have God. He who abides in the doctrine of*
> *Christ has both the Father and the Son. If anyone comes to*
> *you and does not bring this doctrine, do not receive him into*
> *your house nor greet him; for he who greets him shares in his*
> *evil deeds* (2 John 1–2, 4, 7–11).

The "elect lady and her children" to whom John wrote his second letter may have been a particular woman, and John may have been addressing a specific situation. The Greek word translated as lady in this passage is *kuria*, which was a word also used as a proper name in the time of John's letter. It is more likely, however, that John was writing to a body of believers. The church, as the bride of Christ, was often referenced in feminine terminology.

There are two questions that are addressed prominently in 2 John:

1. *What is antichrist?* The use of the word in this passage does not refer to the Antichrist, the embodiment of hatred for and opposition to Christ in the form of one man who arises in the last days. Antichrist means literally *opposite Christ* or *against Christ*. Many beliefs and doctrines are opposed to Christ. Even well-intentioned people can oppose Christ in what they say and do. Jesus said during His earthly ministry, "He who is not with Me is against Me, and he who does not gather with Me scatters abroad" (Matt. 12:30).

Certainly the false teachers who attempted to divert the first-century believers from pure faith in Christ Jesus were antichrist. One does not need to be hateful or angry to be anti-Christ. Teaching anything that is contrary to what Jesus taught and doing anything that is contrary to what Jesus did is *anti*-Christ, even though the teaching may sound good and the deed may appear good on the surface.

In order to determine what is antichrist, a person must first know with great confidence, accuracy, and conviction what is *pro*-Christ or *for*-Christ. If we truly know what honors Christ and exalts Him as the Son of God and our Savior and Lord, then we readily understand what hurts the heart of God, what injures a Christian's testimony, what limits the gospel and damages the kingdom of God, and what fails to draw a person closer to God.

We also must be careful that we do not assume a person is antichrist just because he or she belongs to a denomination that is different than ours. There are many styles of praise and worship, but only one gospel. As Paul wrote to the Ephesians, "There is one body and one Spirit . . . one hope of your calling; one Lord, one faith, one baptism; one God and Father of all" (Eph. 4:4–6). Jesus also made this clear when John came to him on one occasion asking that Jesus forbid someone who was casting out demons in Jesus' name. John asked this because the person was not one of the twelve chosen disciples. Jesus replied, "Do not forbid him, for he who is not against us is on our side" (Luke 9:50).

2. *To whom should hospitality be extended?* The second major question addressed in John's letter dealt with the issue of hospitality, which was very important in the ancient world. The Roman Empire had an extensive network of roads that allowed its citizens to travel freely and widely. Inns were located at twenty-two mile intervals, but the average inn tended to be noisy and dirty. Thieves often stayed at these inns. Travelers generally tried to stay with friends along the way, or with friends of their friends. Christians naturally gravitated toward seeking out and staying with fellow Christians as they traveled, and because of this, a tremendous amount of teaching and edification occurred as Christians shared with Christians what they had been taught or had experienced as they followed the Lord.

More officially, the gospel was also spread by traveling missionaries who were sent out by churches. These missionary teachers, preachers, and evangelists traveled from church to church. Hospitality shown to them was considered a great expression of Christian love (Rom. 12:13; Heb. 13:16). Unfortunately, as the word got out that Christians would feed and house those who claimed to be spreading the gospel, pseudo-missionaries began to appear. Some of these were false teachers. Others were simply travelers who had learned enough of the terminology associated with the believers to pass themselves off as Christians. John admonished the church to put travelers to a test before extending hospitality to them: does the person abide in the doctrine of Christ?

If so, that person was to be treated with great hospitality.

If not, a Christian was under no obligation to extend hospitality. In fact, John said plainly, "Do not receive him into your house nor greet him." To do so was to share in the person's evil.

What was the danger in offering hospitality to a nonbeliever or a false teacher? In the ancient world the sharing of meals and the sharing of lodging meant a sharing of lives. The person extending hospitality to a stranger was responsible for defending that stranger, even to the point of death. To break bread with a person was to say to that person, "You are like my own family." To extend hospitality to an unbeliever or a false teacher was to say, "You are a member of the family of God, the Body of Christ"—which was a lie.

To answer the question about whether a person abides in the doctrine of Christ, a person must first *know* the doctrine of Christ. Doctrine refers to the basic set of principles that comprise one's belief system. The creeds of the ancient church, such as the Apostle's Creed and Nicene Creed, were composed to state the doctrine of Christ in a succinct manner.

Do you know today what is against or opposite Christ?

Do you know today how to evaluate whether a person abides in the doctrine of Christ?

A
Application for Today

Below is the Nicene Creed. As you read through this, ask yourself, "Do I truly believe what this creed expresses?"

> We believe in one God, the Father, the Almighty, maker of heaven and earth, of all that is, seen and unseen.
>
> We believe in one Lord, Jesus Christ, the only Son of God, eternally begotten of the Father, God from God, Light from Light, true God from true God, begotten, not made, of one Being with the Father. Through him all things were made. For us and for our salvation he came down from heaven: by the power of the Holy Spirit he became incarnate from the Virgin Mary, and was made man. For our sake, he was crucified under Pontius Pilate; he suffered death and was buried. On the third day he rose again in accordance with the Scriptures; he ascended into heaven and is seated sat the right hand of the Father. He will come again in glory to judge the living and the dead, and His kingdom will have no end.
>
> We believe in the Holy Spirit, the Lord, the giver of life, who proceeds from the Father and the Son. With the Father and the Son he is worshiped and glorified. He has spoken through the Prophets. We believe in one holy catholic and apostolic Church. We acknowledge one baptism for the forgiveness of sins. We

look for the resurrection of the dead, and the life of the world to come. Amen.

Do you limit your hospitality to those who abide in these truths?

Do you monitor closely those you invite to your home, whether for meals, parties, or overnight lodging?

What is the danger of extending hospitality to those who do not believe in Christ Jesus? In what ways might they lead your children or other family members astray? In what ways is your example of extending meals and lodging to sinners setting an example that it is acceptable to have fellowship with unbelievers outside your home?

S
Supplementary Scriptures to Consider

John also addressed those who were antichrist in his first letter:

> Little children, it is the last hour; and as you have heard that the Antichrist is coming, even now many antichrists have come, by which we know that it is the last hour. They went out from us, but they were not of us; for if they had been of us, they would have continued with us; but they went out that they might be made manifest, that none of them were of us.
>
> But you have an anointing from the Holy One, and you know all things. I have not written to you because you do not know the truth, but because you know it, and that no lie is of the truth.
>
> Who is a liar but he who denies that Jesus is the Christ? He is antichrist who denies the Father and the Son. Whoever denies the Son does not have the Father either; he who acknowledges the Son has the Father also (1 John 2:18–23).

• In what ways can a person rely on the Holy Spirit for discerning those who are antichrist?

- The central questions for discerning those who were antichrist appear to have been, "Is Jesus the Savior? Is Jesus the Son of God?" Why is it important to have answers to these questions before participating in ministry outreaches or evangelistic missions with another person?

- To what extent should we know what a person believes about Christ before we do the following?

    Extend church membership to that person?

    Elevate a person to a position of leadership in the church?

    Allow a person to teach or preach?

    Invite a person to participate in a home fellowship group?

    Allow our children to socialize with their children?

John told the church that it already knew how to tell truth from a lie.

> These things I have written to you concerning those who try to deceive you. But the anointing which you have received from Him abides in you, and you do not need that anyone teach you; but as the same anointing teaches you concerning all things, and is true, and is not a lie, and just as it has taught you, you will abide in Him (1 John 2:26–27).

• When you are in the presence of someone who tells a lie about Jesus or you hear a message that doesn't ring true to the gospel, how do you feel? What do you do in those cases?

In John's third letter he wrote:

> To the beloved Gaius, whom I love in truth:
> Beloved, I pray that you may prosper in all things and be in health, just as your soul prospers. For I rejoiced greatly when brethren came and testified of the truth that is in you, just as you walk in the truth. I have no greater joy than to hear that my children walk in truth (3 John 1–4).

• What does it mean to you to "walk in truth"?

• To what degree is "walking in truth" critical to a person's prosperity (physical, spiritual, and material)?

John clearly understood that deceit and the implementation of antichrist beliefs was the work of the devil:

> We know that we are of God, and the whole world lies under the sway of the wicked one.
> And we know that the Son of God has come and has given us an understanding, that we may know Him who is true; and we are in Him who is true, in His Son Jesus Christ. This is the true God and eternal life (1 John 5:19–20).

• How might a Christian confront the lies told by an unsaved person or false teacher, while still extending the mercy and forgiveness of God to that person?

I
Introspection and Implications

1. How well do you know the mind of Christ? Do you have a good understanding of what Jesus would think, say, or do in situations and circumstances you routinely encounter? How do we develop the mind of Christ?

2. John wrote, "For many deceivers have gone out into the world who do not confess Jesus Christ as coming in the flesh." There were those who taught in the first century that Jesus was only spirit, and not truly the incarnate God. There are those today who say that Jesus never really existed, but that He simply became a spiritual ideal through the centuries. How would you respond to a person who made those statements to you?

3. How would you respond to a person who claimed your lack of in-home hospitality extended to sinners was unloving?

4. Where *should* a person meet and present the gospel of Christ to those who are unbelievers?

5. In what settings *should* a person confront those who are false teachers or who are antichrist?

6. If we are not to extend hospitality to those who do not abide in the doctrine of Christ, are we to *receive* hospitality from those who do not abide in Him? In other words, are we to go to their homes for meals or parties?

C
Communicating the Good News

A number of religious groups send their members door to door to present false doctrines. Many of these groups seek to be invited into a person's home to further present their message. Why is it wise *never* to invite these people into your home? What should a Christian say to them?

To what extent should unbelievers be invited to church social events? Should evangelistic outreaches be in public places? Why or why not?

LESSON #6

IMITATING AND DOING GOOD

Imitate: use someone as a model, attempting to copy their existing method, style, approach, behavior, voice, or message

B
Bible Focus

> Beloved, do not imitate what is evil, but what is good. He
> who does good is of God, but he who does evil has not seen
> God (3 John 11).

John may appear to have been stating the obvious, but fewer passages
in the New Testament are more compelling or more profound in their
simplicity.

First, John made it plain that we all imitate the behavior of others. This
places great responsibility on each of us to choose our role models wisely.
Who do we copy when it comes to our behavior in church? Who do we
imitate when it comes to the way we pray, the way we talk about Jesus, the
way we praise and give thanks to the Lord, or the way we encourage one
another to develop Christ-like character and values? Who do we imitate as
we begin to exercise and develop our spiritual gifts? Who do we copy when
we live out our day to day responsibilities and commitments as parents,
grandparents, aunts and uncles, siblings, workers or employers, friends, and
neighbors?

To a great extent, the person you *choose* as your role model of Christ-like
behavior will be the person you eventually *become* to those who follow you.

Second, John offered no middle ground between evil and good. He
established only two categories of thought, word, and deed: good and evil.
Anything that is "sort of bad" *is* bad. This means that what we think is right
or wrong. What we hold as an attitude is either godly or ungodly. What we
say is either the truth or a lie. What we do is either beneficial to the kingdom
of God or harmful to it.

Third, John said we can know who is godly and who isn't based on
behavior. Listen closely to what a person says. Watch their body language
and facial expressions. See where they go, what they choose, and what they
decide. Monitor their behavior. See how they treat other people when they
know they are being watched and when they think they are *not* being
watched. See how they relate to those who are well-off and to those who are
in need. Watch how they treat little children, the elderly, strangers, widows,
and those who are sick or handicapped.

While we are admonished never to judge or condemn another person, we
are to judge behavior. We are to know with certainty what is right and
wrong, true and untrue, good and bad. We are the ones who determine which
behaviors we will copy and which behaviors we will reject as being totally
unsuitable for us as Christ-followers.

Fourth, John said that the only criterion that really counts is knowing and
doing what is *good*.

In our world today, a great deal of emphasis is placed on whether certain deeds, decisions, or programs are efficient, effective, strategic, significant, timely, organized, productive, influential, and so forth. While those attributes are good gauges at certain times for various reasons, ultimately we only need to know if something is *good.*

A thought, word, or deed is only *good* if God says it is good. We need to read and study the Scriptures with an eye always to what God approves, what God declares as permissible and desirable, what God rewards, and what God considers to be worthy of His blessing.

The pursuit of anything other than what God calls good is a waste of time, energy, and resources.

In what ways do we look to human standards to define goodness, rather than focus on God's standards? How can we begin to evaluate *all* things in our lives according to what God says about them?

A
Application for Today

A woman met one of her neighbors in the grocery store and was surprised when her neighbor said, "I have news that you will probably enjoy hearing."

"What is it?" the woman asked.

"I went to the citywide evangelistic rally down at the civic center last weekend, and I went forward to accept Jesus as my Savior!"

"That's wonderful!" the woman replied. "I truly am thrilled to hear this news! Thank you for telling me. But I'm also curious, why did you think I would enjoy knowing this?"

"Oh," the neighbor said, "I know you go to church. I have watched you drive by my window on Sunday mornings."

The woman smiled inwardly. She had never really thought about her driving to church on Sundays as being a form of witness for Christ.

"Why don't you go with me to church next Sunday?" the woman suggested warmly.

"I'm not sure I'd know what to do," the neighbor said. "I haven't been to too many church services, usually just weddings and funerals. I might embarrass you by what I say or do."

"Never!" the woman said. "Here's the key: watch me and do what I do. If I mess up, we both mess up. That way, neither one of us can be embarrassed!"

We each learn how to behave in church by imitating others, perhaps by imitating our parents when we were children, perhaps by imitating our friends who first invited us to church.

To what degree are we each responsible for leading or training up those who are new converts to Christ Jesus?

In what ways are we each challenged to model Christ before those who don't know Christ?

S
Supplementary Scriptures to Consider

In his letters, John made a number of statements about what leads to good behavior:

> Little children, keep yourselves from idols (1 John 5:21).

- An idol, according to Scripture, is anything a person trusts in any way, about any aspect of his life, equal to or more than the person trusts God. What are the most common idols in twenty-first century, developed nations?

- Have you ever had an idol? Do you still? What happened?

- In what ways is it difficult for a person to recognize his or her own idols?

Most people consider prayer to be something *good* in God's eyes. John called upon the church to be bold in prayer:

> Now this is the confidence that we have in Him, that if we ask anything according to His will, He hears us. And if we know that He hears us, whatever we ask, we know that we have the petitions that we have asked of Him (1 John 5:14–15).

- In what ways can we know that we are asking God for things that are "according to His will"?

- How do we determine if what we are requesting from God will turn out to be genuinely *good* for us?

- Does God *hear* petitions in prayer that will result in any taint of evil? Does He answer those prayers as the person praying usually desires?

John also wrote this about doing what is good:

> We know that whoever is born of God does not sin; but he
> who has been born of God keeps himself, and the wicked one
> does not touch him (1 John 5:18).

- What does it mean in very practical concrete terms for a person to "keep" himself? (Note: to *keep* means *to set restraints, to limit, to guard*.)

- How does this statement by John relate to James' assurance that when we resist the devil, he must flee from us (James 4:7)?

Concerning knowing what is good, John wrote:

> Beloved, do not believe every spirit, but test the spirits,
> whether they are of God; because many false prophets have
> gone out into the world. By this you know the Spirit of God:
> every spirit that confesses that Jesus Christ has come in the
> flesh is of God, and every spirit that does not confess that
> Jesus Christ has come in the flesh is not of God. And this is
> the spirit of the Antichrist, which you have heard was coming,
> and is now already in the world (1 John 4:1–3).

- The philosophy that John was addressing contended that God would never stoop to entering the practical everyday world. The gospel declared that Jesus was God incarnate. He not only stooped to enter humanity but He died for the sins of humanity. Those who are Christians proclaim that the same Spirit that indwelled Christ Jesus now indwells them. They are human vessels bearing the Spirit of Christ into the world. The criterion for testing the spirits today may be stated this way: "Can I confess Jesus is the Christ as I do this?" What are things you *cannot* do and still profess that Jesus is your Savior?

• What do you say to the person who declares, "You can do anything you want because God doesn't really care what you *do*. He only cares about what you believe"?

John assured the church that it could rely on the Holy Spirit to help believers choose and live out what is *good*:

> You are of God, little children, and have overcome them, because He who is in you is greater than he who is in the world. They are of the world. Therefore they speak as of the world, and the world hears them. We are of God. He who knows God hears us; he who is not of God does not hear us. By this we know the spirit of truth and the spirit of error (1 John 4:4–6).

• What does it mean to you that "He [the Holy Spirit] who is in you is greater than he [the devil] who is in the world"?

• Why is it impossible for an unsaved person to really hear the gospel of Jesus Christ apart from the Holy Spirit dealing with their heart and convicting the person of the truth being presented to them?

• In what ways do we need to rely on the Holy Spirit daily to give us ears to hear the truth, to believe what is right, and to choose what is good?

I
Introspection and Implications

1. Have you ever tried to justify your behavior as *good* even when you knew it wasn't? What was the outcome?

2. Do you have a good understanding of what God calls *good*? How can you grow in that understanding?

3. Below, identify *whom* you have chosen as a role model in each of these areas, and then make a brief statement as to *why:*

Area of Behavior	Who	Why
Parenting skills		
Displaying true friendship		
Spiritual giftedness		
Faithfulness to Christ		
Bold witness for Christ		
Prayer		
Giving to the church		
Loving others		
Studying God's Word		

C
Communicating the Good News

How would you respond to a person who said, "I'm not good enough to be a Christian"?

LESSON #7

CONTENDING FOR THE FAITH

Contend: compete for something; to debate, argue, dispute, or struggle against all who deny the truth of Christ Jesus

B
Bible Focus

Jude, a bondservant of Jesus Christ, and brother of James,
To those who are called, sanctified by God the Father, and
preserved in Jesus Christ:
Mercy, peace, and love be multiplied to you.
Beloved, while I was very diligent to write to you concern-
ing our common salvation, I found it necessary to write to you
exhorting you to contend earnestly for the faith which was
once for all delivered to the saints. For certain men have crept
in unnoticed, who long ago were marked out for this condem-
nation, ungodly men, who turn the grace of our God into
lewdness and deny the only Lord God and our Lord Jesus
Christ. . . .
These are spots in your love feasts, while they feast with
you without fear, serving only themselves. They are clouds
without water, carried about by the winds; late autumn trees
without fruit, twice dead, pulled up by the roots; raging waves
of the sea, foaming up their own shame; wandering stars for
whom is reserved the blackness of darkness forever
(Jude 1–4; 12–13).

Like John and other New Testament writers, Jude was acutely aware of
the false teachers who were leading believers astray, and he took a strong
stand against them. His letter has some of the most vivid and most stinging
language in the Scriptures.

Note how Jude began his letter. He affirmed the recipients of his message
and described them in three ways:

- *Called.* Jude, like the other New Testament writers, believed that those
  who followed Christ had been chosen to do so—but with this understanding: the called are those who have accepted God's calling to them, and the
  chosen are those who choose to be chosen.

- *Sanctified.* To be sanctified is to be cleansed and set apart for God's
  purposes.

- *Preserved in Jesus Christ.* Those who have not wavered in times of
  persecution but who have withstood suffering and remained faithful are
  preserved in Christ.

These are the ones whom Jude challenges to "contend earnestly for the
faith"! Jude was not asking new or immature believers to take on the false

teachers. However, he expected that those who were strong and mature would not only confront false teachers but prevail in driving them from the church. We must recognize that there are some tasks in the discipline of the church that are the direct responsibility of those who are spiritually mature, and we must be careful in asking immature believers to contend for the faith when they are not yet able to do so victoriously. This does not mean that new believers cannot engage in evangelism of the lost. It does mean that new believers are not yet equipped, by an understanding of the Word or by experience in walking consistently with the Lord, to take on those who are ungodly but have assumed leadership positions in the church.

Jude said this in his opening words: "Mercy, peace, and love" be multiplied to you."

- Mercy is a spirit of forgiveness toward those who do not deserve it, an expression of compassion for those who need help.

- Peace is harmony that leads to growth, healing, wholeness, and the perfection of goodness.

- Love is giving to others all that God has given to His forgiven and beloved children.

These attributes are to mark the behavior of all Christians, especially the words and behavior of those who contend for the faith. We are never to take on false teachers or evil influencers with an attitude of anger or condemnation. At all times we are to seek to restore those who are wandering away from Christ, to bring back to the truth those who are pursuing a lie, and to bring about reconciliation in Christ with those who are aligning themselves with evil.

We are to contend earnestly—sincere, ardent, and unrelenting, but never with malice.

Jude called upon those who contend for the faith to clearly understanding that their enemies:

- Serve only themselves. They are totally focused on self.

- Clouds without water, carried about by the winds. They are empty inside and highly susceptible to suggestion.

- Late autumn trees without fruit, twice dead, pulled up by the roots—they produce nothing that is genuinely beneficial and spiritually nourishing, and they have no real source of spiritual benefit or nourishment for their own lives.

- Raging waves of the sea, foaming up their own shame. They are all froth and no substance, seemingly powerful, but only on the surface. They have no depth of character or real authority born of deep conviction or values.

- Wandering stars. They are not genuine stars but rather comets and meteors that will eventually burn out and burn up.

Jude called upon the contenders to see the weaknesses of the false teachers and to address those weaknesses. Knowing one's enemy is the first step in defeating the enemy. When you discover where a person is hurting or lacking, you can present Christ as the one who heals and provides what is missing.

Jude told the church *who* should do the contending, *how* they should contend, and *where* they should focus their message.

We are wise to follow his exhortation as we encounter those who seek to destroy the church in our world.

Are you a qualified contender?

Do you have a godly spiritual attitude as you take on the enemies of the faith?

Do you know the weaknesses of your enemies and how to speak to those weaknesses in the strength of the Holy Spirit?

If so, consider yourself exhorted to *contend*!

A
Application for Today

A young teenager arrived home in a huff. "I am sick and tired of all the debates that I have to listen to at school," he said to his father.

"Debates about what?" Dad asked.

"Two weeks ago we had a debate about evolution in my biology class. Last week we got into a debate in my history class about whether war is ever justifiable. Yesterday we got into a debate in my health class about abortion. Today I had to listen to everybody in my political science class debate about capital punishment. I don't even want to think about what might come up tomorrow."

"Are you speaking up during these debates?" Dad asked.

"Sometimes I do," the teen said. "But Dad, some of the time I don't know what to say—I don't have enough facts. I don't have my arguments all thought out. And most of the time, I don't speak up because I don't think that anything I say will really make a difference. Those who have their minds made up *really* seem to have their minds made up . . . to the point their minds are closed!"

If you were this boy's parent, how would you respond?

In what ways do you have your arguments lined up for the gospel? Do you need to prepare yourself more fully?

Are there issues a Christian can debate and win?

When should we take the approach Jude advised: speak to those who are in error by saying, "The Lord rebuke you!"?

S
Supplementary Scriptures to Consider

Jude wrote very plainly that it is possible for people to rebel in a way that shuts them out of God's blessing:

> But I want to remind you, though you once knew this, that the Lord, having saved the people out of the land of Egypt, afterward destroyed those who did not believe. And the angels who did not keep their proper domain, but left their own abode, He has reserved in everlasting chains under darkness for the judgment of the great day; as Sodom and Gomorrah, and the cities around them in a similar manner to these, having given themselves over to sexual immorality and gone after strange flesh, are set forth as an example, suffering the vengeance of eternal fire (Jude 5–7).

- What might be keeping you from the fullness of blessing that God desires for you? What might be keeping your church from the fullness of blessing that God has for those who are His faithful children? As you are able to identify the areas of sin that block the flow of God's rewards what must you do?

Jude admonished those who contended for the faith to do so in a specific way:

> Likewise also these dreamers defile the flesh, reject authority, and speak evil of dignitaries. Yet Michael the archangel, in contending with the devil, when he disputed about the body of Moses, dared not bring against him a reviling accusation, but said, "The Lord rebuke you!" But these speak evil of whatever they do not know; and whatever they know naturally, like brute beasts, in these things they corrupt themselves. Woe to them! For they have gone in the way of Cain, have run greedily in the error of Balaam for profit, and perished in the rebellion of Korah (Jude 8–11).

• What does it mean to refrain from bringing "reviling accusation"?

• We are not to become *like* those who defile the flesh, reject authority, or speak evil of dignitaries. But at the same time, we are to rebuke them. How do we confront the enemies of the faith without stooping to their tactics or using their methods?

• Jude referred to three well-known incidents described in the Old Testament. You may want to reread these passages: Genesis 4:1–10, Numbers 22–24, and Numbers 16. Cain killed his brother in a rage of jealousy. Balaam was willing to give false prophecy for money. Korah led a group of Israelites in rebellion against Moses in an attempt to assume leadership power. What traits was Jude calling upon the church to recognize in those he called ungodly?

Jude encouraged the church to remember that the host of heaven was on their side!

> Now Enoch, the seventh from Adam, prophesied about these men also, saying, "Behold, the Lord comes with ten thousands of His saints, to execute judgment on all, to convict all who are ungodly among them of all their ungodly deeds which they have committed in an ungodly way, and of all the harsh things which ungodly sinners have spoken against Him" (Jude 14–15).

• How do you remind yourself of who is on *your* side of righteousness? Why is it important to remind yourself often of this?

Jude described those who must be confronted in the church:

> These are grumblers, complainers, walking according to their own lusts; and they mouth great swelling words, flattering people to gain advantage. But you, beloved, remember the words which were spoken before by the apostles of our Lord Jesus Christ: how they told you that there would be mockers in the last time who would walk according to their own ungodly lusts. These are sensual persons, who cause divisions, not having the Spirit (Jude 16–19).

- What is the behavior associated with grumbling? Complaining? Walking according to one's own lusts?

- Have you ever encountered someone who used "great swelling words" to flatter people and gain advantage? What did you do? What was the outcome?

- What is *your* description or definition of a mocker? (Note: one dictionary defines mockery as using ridicule to make something appear silly or inadequate). Have you ever dealt with someone who was a mocker of the faith? What did you do?

Jude also admonished the church to do four things:

> But you, beloved, building yourselves up on your most holy faith, praying in the Holy Spirit, keep yourselves in the love of God, looking for the mercy of our Lord Jesus Christ unto eternal life (Jude 20–21).

• What does it mean to you, in practical everyday terms, to build yourself up on your most holy faith?

• What does it mean to pray in the Holy Spirit?

• What does it mean to keep yourself in the love of God?

• How do you look for the "mercy of Jesus Christ unto eternal life"?

• How are these the acts of contending for the faith?

I
Introspection and Implications

1. Are you a qualified contender for the faith? If you do not believe you are, how can you become qualified to be a contender?

2. What does it mean to you for the faith to have been "once for all delivered to the saints"? Is there anything about the truth of the gospel that is subject to change according to innovations of technology or alterations in human customs and cultures?

3. How do you struggle to have your speech and actions reflect God's mercy, peace, and love?

C
Communicating the Good News

Why must we avoid being contentious or combative as we present the gospel?

How might our evangelistic messages be couched in terms that express even *more* of God's

Mercy:

Peace:

Love:

NOTES TO LEADERS
OF SMALL GROUPS

A s the leader of a small discussion group, think of yourself as a facilitator with three main roles:

- Get the discussion started.

- Involve every person in the group.

- Encourage an open, candid discussion that remains Bible-focused.

You certainly don't need to be the person with all the answers! In truth, much of your role is to be a person who asks questions:

- What really impacted you most in this lesson?

- Was there a particular part of the lesson or a question that you found troubling?

- Was there a particular part of the lesson that you found encouraging or insightful?

- Was there a particular part of the lesson that you'd like to explore further?

Express to the group at the outset of your study that your goal as a group is to gain new insights into God's Word; this is not the forum for defending a point of doctrine or a theological opinion. Stay focused on what God's Word says and means. The purpose of the study is also to share insights on how to apply God's Word to everyday life. *Every* person in the group can and should contribute. The collective wisdom that flows from Bible-focused discussion is often very rich and deep.

Seek to create an environment in which every member of the group feels free to ask questions of other members in order to gain greater understanding. Encourage the group members to voice their appreciation to one another for new insights gained and to be supportive of one another personally. Take the lead in doing this. Genuinely appreciate and value the contributions made by each person.

Since the letters of John and Jude are geared to our personal Christian lives as well as to the life of the church as a whole, you may experience a tendency in your group sessions to become overly critical of your *own* church or church leaders. Avoid the tendency to create discord or dissatisfaction. Don't use this Bible study as an opportunity to spread rumors, air someone's dirty laundry, or criticize your pastor. Rather, seek positive ways to build up one another, including your church leaders. Seek positive outcomes and solutions to any problems you may identify.

You may want to begin each study by having one or more members of the group read through the section provided under "Bible Focus." Ask the group specifically if it desires to discuss any of the questions under the "Application" section, the "Supplemental Scriptures" section, and the "Implications" and "Communicating the gospel" sections. You do not need to bring closure—or come to a definitive conclusion or consensus—about any one question asked in this study. Rather, if the group does not *have* a satisfactory Bible-based answer to a question, encourage them to engage in further "ask, seek, and knock" strategies to discover the answers! Remember the words of Jesus: "Ask, and it will be given to you, seek, and you will find; knock, and it will be opened to you. For everyone who asks receives, and he who seeks finds, and to him who knocks it will be opened" (Matt. 7:7–8).

Finally, open and close your study with prayer. Ask the Holy Spirit, whom Jesus called the Spirit of Truth, to guide your discussion and to reveal what is of eternal benefit to you individually and as a group. As you close your study, ask the Holy Spirit to seal to your remembrance what you have read and studied and to show you ways in the upcoming days, weeks, and months *how* to apply what you have studied to your daily life and relationships.

General Themes for the Lessons

Each lesson in this study has one or more core themes. Continually pull the group back to these themes. You can do this by asking simple questions, such as, "How is that related to _____?" or "How does that help us better understand the concept of *Blackaby Study Bible*?" . . . "In what ways does that help us apply the principle of _____?"

A summary of general themes or concepts in each lesson is provided below:

Lesson #1
FELLOWSHIP WITH THE TRUE LIGHT
Discerning which messages are right before God, and which are not
The sinful nature of all human beings
Confession and forgiveness
Fellowship with God and other people

Lesson #2
THE LOVE OF THE FATHER BESTOWED ON US
God's love`
Our response to God's love
God's love flowing through us to others

Lesson #3
DEALING WITH SIN
Jesus our Advocate
Our ability to live without sin

Lesson #4
THE PERFECTING OF LOVE
Examples of sacrificial love
Practical examples of love shown to others—believers, unbelievers
Fears about expressing love

Lesson #5
WALKING IN THE TRUTH OF CHRIST
The spirit of antichrist
Extending hospitality

Lesson #6
IMITATING AND DOING GOOD
God's definition of "good"
Choosing good role models
Helping your children choose good role models
Relying on the Holy Spirit for discernment of what is good
Relying on the Holy Spirit for help in doing and saying what is good

Lesson #7

CONTENDING FOR THE FAITH

What it means to contend

Who should contend for the faith

What the spiritual attitude of those who contend for the faith should be

How to contend effectively

How to build ourselves up so we might become victorious contenders

NOTES

NOTES